# GONE FOREVER

# THE
# LOST PARROTS
# OF AMERICA

by Terry Dunnahoo

CRESTWOOD HOUSE

New York

## LIBRARY OF CONGRESS CATALOGING IN PUBLICATION DATA

Dunnahoo, Terry
  The lost parrots of America / by Terry Dunnahoo

  p. cm. (Gone forever)
  Includes index.
  SUMMARY: Discusses the extinction of several species of parrots, including the Carolina Parakeet and the Cuban Red Macaw.
  1. Parrots – North America – Juvenile literature. 2. Birds, Extinct – North America – Juvenile literature. 3. Birds, Protection of – North America – Juvenile literature. [1. Parrots. 2. Extinct birds.] I. Title. II. Series.
QL696.P7D86        1989        598'.71 – dc20        89-7846
ISBN 0-89686-461-8                               CIP
                                                       AC

# *Photo Credits*

DRK Photo: (Stephen J. Krasemann) 5, 14, 17, 18, 32; (Wayne Lynch) 6; (Don & Pat Valenti) 9; (Belinda Wright) 10; (C. C. Lockwood) 12; (Larry Lipsky) 15, 16, 38; (R. J. Erwin) 20; (Jeff Foott) 44; (M. P. Kahl) 45
Photo Researchers, Inc.: 28; (Audubon Society) 29; (Will & Deni McIntrye) 11; (Tom McHugh) 30
Academy of Natural Sciences: ( J. Dunning) 22, 40; (Sid Lipschutz) 42
Steven Holt: 26
The Bettmann Archive: 35
Wide World Photos, Inc.: 24

Cover illustration by Kristi Schaeppi

Consultant: Professor Robert E. Sloan, Paleontologist
University of Minnesota

Macmillan Publishing Company
866 Third Avenue
New York, NY 10022
Collier Macmillan Canada, Inc.

CRESTWOOD HOUSE
Produced by Carnival Enterprises

Printed in the United States of America

First Edition

10 9 8 7 6 5 4 3 2 1

# Contents

North America

South America

*Most of the parrots in this book were found throughout North, Central, and South America.*

*The Carolina Parakeet, the only parrot native to the United States, is now extinct.*

# Parrots and Pirates

The pictures in pirate books almost always show pirates with parrots on their shoulders. The typical pirate has a peg leg and a patch over one eye. He is usually stealing somebody else's gold. Not all pirates had peg legs or eye patches, of course. But many of them did keep parrots. Parrots make very loyal pets.

Parrots have been friends to humans for thousands of years. Parrots were kept as pets in China and India. The people loved parrots for their beauty and ability to "talk."

Parrots were brought to Europe from India by Alexander the Great. The Greeks and the Romans soon loved parrots for the same reasons. They were the most popular caged birds in the ancient world.

Parrots were not only kept as pets, they were also kept for food. One Roman emperor even fed parrot heads to his lions. Sometimes he served parrot heads to his guests! As a special treat he gave them parrot tongues.

Natives of North and South America also ate parrots. Some explorers who came to the Americas ate them, too. Christopher Columbus brought parrots to Spain after his first voyage. He paraded in front of Queen Isabella and King Ferdinand with a parrot on his arm.

Explorers began to tell stories about parrots. One man who sailed with Columbus said parrots helped them find land. One day, a flock of parrots stayed with the *Niña*, the *Pinta,* and the *Santa Maria* until late afternoon. Then they flew away. The ships followed the parrots and found land – or so the sailor said.

Another tale about parrots was told in early Panama. One morning in 1509, parrots screamed and squawked, waking an entire village. The squawking parrots warned the vil-lagers that the Spaniards were about to attack. The warning gave the villagers time to escape into the jungle.

Each of these stories sounds fantastic. But they all show how much people love parrots. These colorful birds have become part of America's history.

# The Evolution of Birds

Where did birds come from? One theory says birds *evolved* from dinosaurs. Their scales changed to feathers over millions of years.

The oldest bird *fossil* ever found was of a bird the size of a chicken. It lived about 150 million years ago. This bird had feathers. But the skull, eyes, and teeth were still like those of reptiles. Seventy-five million years ago most birds looked like birds we see today.

Many millions of years ago the earth looked different than it does today. The continents were not where you see them on a globe. They have moved. South America, Africa, Australia, and Antarctica were one giant land mass. Some scientists believe birds evolved in one area and spread to the other continents.

The family of birds we call parrots probably evolved around 30 million years ago. Parrots lived in South America, Australia, and Africa. Different *species* of parrots spread to Central America, too.

A parrot fossil was even discovered in Nebraska. The fossil was 20 million years old. That means some parrots lived in North America long ago.

One parrot that lived in North America was called the Carolina Parakeet. Parakeets are a species of small parrots with slender tails. The Carolina Parakeet, sadly, is now *extinct*. It is gone forever.

8 *The Carolina Parakeet used to fly in flocks of 200 to 300 birds. It was only 12 inches long.*

*The Rose Ringed Parakeet of India is one member of the Psittacidae family.*

# One Happy Family

Scientists classify birds into families. The family of parrots is called *Psittacidae*. There are more than 300 species in this family. The word "parrot" is correctly used to identify birds in the Psittacidae family. But some are usually known by their more popular names. These include macaws, parakeets, cockatoos, and lories.

Parrots seem to come in all sizes. The Pygmy Parrot of Papua is only three and one half inches long from its beak to the end of its tail. Some macaws in South America, however, are over three feet long.

*This print of an extinct Carolina Parakeet shows why parrots are grouped into the same family. All parrots have two toes that point forward and two that point backward.*

Parrots come in many different colors. Most commonly a parrot's feathers are largely green. Some parrots also have large red, yellow, and blue feathers. A few parrots are black. Some are white with small, colored feathers.

If many parrots look different, why do they belong to the same family? They are in the same family mainly because they have certain body traits in common.

For example, the feet of all parrots are similar – they are all *zygodactyl*. This means each foot has two toes that point forward and two that point backward. Parrots use their feet and beaks to climb. They also use their feet to

hold food. They bite off pieces of food as though they were eating a sandwich.

Beaks of parrots are also similar. A parrot's beak is large and curved like a hook. The beak is hinged so that the top and bottom halves of the beak can move separately. This helps parrots get seeds out of shells and open them. When the beak is closed, the top half fits over the bottom half.

The shape of a parrot's beak varies with its diet. The beaks of parrots that feed on nuts and hard-shelled fruits are curved the most. Parrots that feed on roots have longer, straighter beaks. Parrots that feed on nectar from flowers have narrow beaks.

Parrots often use their beaks like a third foot. They grab a branch with their beaks and step up or down. This allows them to move quickly through the trees to find food.

In the wild, parrots *molt,* or shed their feathers, over several months of the year. Few feathers are lost at the same time, so parrots can fly well even while they are molting. They can still escape from their enemies and gather food.

Parrots have two kinds of feathers: *contour feathers* and *down feathers.* Contour feathers are like overcoats. They can be seen easily. Down feathers are under the contour feathers. Down feathers, like underwear, lie beneath the outer layer and cannot be seen easily.

Unlike most birds, parrots also have *powder-down feathers.* Powder-down feathers break apart into fine

*A Yucatán Parrot of Mexico uses its curved beak to eat an almond.*

Parrots grab onto branches with their beaks in order to move quickly through trees.

Macaws have bright, colorful feathers.

*The large head and short body of the parrot sets it apart from other types of birds.*

powder. Parrots use this powder to clean their feathers. The powder gives feathers color and shine.

Parrots share other traits. Their heads are large in proportion to their bodies. Their necks are short and their tongues are thick and fleshy.

A few parrots live in cold areas. For instance, Keas live in the mountains of New Zealand. Sometimes they even roll in the snow. But most parrots live in tropical and subtropical areas. These places are warm and have a lot of rain. In the Americas, parrots are the most numerous in South America.

*Powder-down feathers crumble into a fine dust. Parrots use it to give contour feathers color and shine.*

# Nesting and Laying Eggs

Most parrots nest in holes in trees. These holes have usually been made by woodpeckers or other birds. After these birds move out, parrots move in. They may enlarge the holes with their beaks, but few parrots make fresh holes in trees.

Some parrots move into termite or ant mounds. And a few parrots actually build their own nests. They build among rocks or in canyon walls. Monk Parakeets are the only parrots that build nests in the open.

When their nesting habitats are destroyed, parrots must move to another location to survive.

Wherever they make their nests, few parrots line them before laying eggs. They are laid on the rotting wood or dirt, with no special covering.

Nest areas in the wild are difficult to reach. This makes parrots hard to observe. Therefore, we know little about the nesting habits and *incubation* of parrots. Most of what we do know comes from studying them in captivity.

During laying season, eggs are usually laid every other day. They are small and white. The number varies from two to five. Sometimes the smaller birds lay as many as eight eggs. The *nestlings* stay close to their parents until they are large enough to venture out on their own.

# Causes of Extinction

Parrots began dying out when more and more people began to settle in North and South America.

This is what is happening today in South America. The ideal home or *habitat* for parrots used to be the rain forests of the Amazon Valley in Brazil. Now large forest areas have been cut down. Houses, roads, and industries have replaced the forests. This has destroyed many nesting areas for parrots. Some parrots have moved to the mountains to nest and feed. Others moved to other areas in South America. In time, they may *adapt* to their new homes.

Parrots that live on islands cannot always fly to safe land. Therefore, the destruction of parrots' homes is more

serious on islands than it is on continents. Parrots that live on the islands near Central America are in special danger. In time, they may become extinct.

Parrots' popularity as pets has also *endangered* them. They are popular because they are pretty. They can also learn to "speak." They do not imitate other birds or animals in the wild. But in captivity some learn to imitate the human voice. The African Parrot in particular has a reputation as a talker. The *Guinness Book of World Records* says an African Grey named Prudle has a vocabulary of 1,000 words.

Amazona Parrots may never learn 1,000 words. But they are some of the best talkers among South American parrots. That's why large numbers were taken for the pet trade. Now Amazonas are in danger of becoming extinct.

The United States imports thousands of birds from South America and Central America every year. This is believed to cause the death of millions of parrots. Many are killed when people cut down trees to get to the nests. Not all nestlings survive the tree crashes. Those that survive are put in cages. Many more parrots die in jungle cages while waiting for buyers. The hunters sell the surviving parrots to traders for a few cents.

Thousands more, crowded together in cages, die on the trip to the United States.

*Amazona Parrots make popular pets because they are good talkers.*

In the early 1930s, this trade was stopped for a few years when a disease was found in parrots brought to the United States. The disease was called *psittacosis* because it was first noticed in parrots. When the disease was discovered in other birds, the name was changed to *ornithosis*. A law was passed to ban new parrots and birds from the United States. When antibiotics reduced the serious danger of the disease, the ban was lifted in 1937. Now all birds coming legally to the United States are held in *quarantine*.

A quarantined parrot is kept separate from other birds for at least 30 days. Parrots that show signs of disease are destroyed. If they are not diseased, they are allowed into the country. Most are sold as pets.

Hunters kill millions of parrots every year when they try to capture the birds to sell as pets.

Parrots are also destroyed by farmers because the birds eat some crops. The farmer sees the parrot as an enemy and destroys its nest.

Parrots are also poisoned accidently with man-made pesticides and herbicides. When birds eat food sprayed with these chemicals, they are poisoned as the chemicals enter their bodies.

Parrots have also been hunted for food and for their feathers. Sometimes they are still hunted for food, but it is now against the law to use most bird feathers for fashions, ceremonies, decorations, and souvenirs.

The lyrics of this song suggest why:

> Yankee Doodle went to town
> Riding on a pony,
> Stuck a feather in his hat
> And called it macaroni.

Many people stuck feathers in their hats over the centuries. But feathers on clothes became wildly popular in the 1700s. Feathers were used to decorate hats, capes, boas, dresses, muffs, and fans. Women also wore them in their hair. Some wore whole stuffed birds on their heads!

The fad continued in the next century. It is estimated that in the 1800s as many as five million birds were killed each year for fashion feathers. One man said he saw feathers from at least 40 species of birds on hats. He saw these in one day on Fifth Avenue in New York City.

By the late 1890s, the killing of birds for their feathers had become a slaughter. Hunters would shoot the birds, then tear the feathers off and leave the bodies.

People finally became angry. They made fun of those who wore feathers. The Audubon Society worked to get laws passed to stop the killings. They even hired people to watch for feather hunters. Two of their workers were killed by *poachers* while on duty in Florida. Poachers are hunters who kill government-protected wildlife.

The use of feathers for ceremonies, decorations, and souvenirs is now limited. The use of feathers from some birds is banned altogether. This has saved some species that had come close to extinction.

Parrots die from illness or old age, just like people and other animals. They also die from natural disasters. Drought takes away their food and they die of starvation. Their nests are destroyed by floods or fires. They die from attacks by larger birds and animals. They die from extreme changes in weather.

These natural disasters do not cause the extinction of a species, however. Usually people cause the extinction of a species.

# *The Carolina Parakeet*

The Carolina Parakeet is thought to be the only member of the parrot family native to the United States. Carolina Parakeets had mostly green feathers. The upper parts of their heads were orange. The rest of the head and the upper half of the neck were yellow. The wings were tinged with olive green and had yellow feathers. Carolina

*In a 1938 fashion show, these students wore costumes of the 1800s, which included hats that were decorated with bird feathers.*

Parakeets were about 12 inches long. They were about the size of a mourning dove.

Carolina Parakeets lived mostly in Florida, North Carolina, and South Carolina. But they ranged over the eastern half of the United States to the Mississippi River. They also ranged from the Gulf of Mexico to New York and the southern coast of the Great Lakes. Few parrots can survive the cold in some of these areas. But temperatures did not cause their extinction. The arrival of humans did.

Before colonists came from Europe, Carolina Parakeets fed on seeds and wild plants. When colonists planted their crops and fruit trees, Carolina Parakeets ate those, too. They especially liked pears, apples, and grapes. They also destroyed haystacks. A flock of parrots would eat the hay. The stacks looked like they were covered by a green, orange, and yellow carpet.

Often there were 200 to 300 birds together. Farmers could kill 20 with one shotgun blast. The noise would scare the others away. But not for long. The survivors would return to hover over the dead and wounded. They, too, would be killed. Hundreds would die in a few hours.

The famous bird artist John James Audubon did not kill them. But in 1831 he wrote that in a few hours he had filled baskets with dead Carolina Parakeets. He used them to make sketches and paint pictures of them.

That same year Audubon wrote: "Our parakeets are very rapidly diminished in number; and in some districts where twenty-five years ago they were plentiful, scarcely

*Famers killed hundreds of Carolina Parakeets in a matter of hours. The birds used to destroy their fruit trees and hay.*

John James Audubon, founder of the Audubon Society, often
sketched Carolina Parakeets.

*An Audubon Society print shows Carolina Parakeets nesting in a tree.*

lived wild in the United States. These
brightly colored foot-long parrots fed on
cocklebur and the farmer's ripening fruit.
They used hollow trees for nesting and roosting.
No one will ever know much about their
lives because during the 1800's they fell victim
to changing habitat and shooting.
The last known Carolina parakeet
was Incas. Like Martha he died here.
The date was February 21, 1918. Except
for the Cincinnati Zoo these two
American birds would not have sur-
vived as long as they did.
AMERICAN PARROT, LIKE
PIGEON, TO BE EXTINCT
FAR-FAMED LAST PARRAKEET OF
TS KIND IS MOURNED AT ZOO
Stephan, Superintendent of the Garden, Believes That Grief Was a Contributing Cause — Will Have the Body Stuffed.
CAROLINA
PARRAKEE
Conurus Carolinen
SOUTHERN STAT

*An exhibit at the Cincinnati Zoo, where the last Carolina Parakeet lived and died, is now on display.*

any are to be seen–I should think that along the Mississippi there is not now half the number that existed fifteen years ago.''

The flocks soon became small groups or a single bird. More birds were dying than were being born. The Carolina Parakeet was on its way to extinction.

When bird collectors learned this was happening, they trapped the birds. Some wanted them because they were rare. Some wanted them to breed. The people who wanted to breed Carolina Parakeets hoped breeding would keep them from becoming extinct. They were not successful.

By the early 1900s, Carolina Parakeets had nearly vanished. One was collected in the wild in Florida in April 1901. In 1904 an *ornithologist,* or bird expert, named Frank Chapman recorded a flock of 13 birds near Lake Okeechobee in Florida. Other sightings were reported in the 1930s. But ornithologists are not sure that the birds reported in the 1930s were Carolina parakeets.

Eventually only a pair was left, and they were too old to breed. They were named Lady Jane and Incas. Both birds were cage mates in the Cincinnatti Zoo for over 30 years. Lady Jane died in 1917. Incas died on February 21, 1918.

# Other Extinct Parrots

Many other types of parrots are extinct. The Cuban Red Macaw is one of them. This macaw lived on Cuba and on the Isle of Pines in the Caribbean. Some of these macaws were probably brought to Spain by Christopher Columbus after his first voyage to the Americas.

The Cuban Red Macaw may also have lived on Guadeloupe. Columbus's son Ferdinand recorded that red parrots on Guadeloupe were "as big as chickens." Some ornithologists believe he was writing about the Cuban Red Macaw.

Cuban Red Macaws were mostly red. The tops of their heads were tinged with yellow. Feathers on their upper backs were brownish red with some green feathers. The lower back feathers were blue. Their throat feathers were

31

CUBAN MACAW

INHABITED CUBA AND THE ISL
HE LAST KNOWN SPECIMEN WAS
HE OF THE RAREST BIRDS; LESS
-PECIMENS IN THE MUSEUMS OF

**EXTINCT**

*The Cuban Red Macaw is only one of many different macaws that are now extinct.*

orange-red. The tails were tipped with blue. They were approximately 20 inches long.

Most of what we know about Cuban Red Macaws comes from Dr. J. Gundlach. Dr. Gundlach wrote that, in 1849, Cuban Red Macaws could be easily found. He also wrote that the Cuban natives trapped and shot them for food. He said the meat had a foul smell and tasted terrible, but the natives ate it anyway. Natives also cut down trees to get birds for pets. Those actions led to the extinction of the Cuban Red Macaw.

According to Gundlach, the last recorded shooting of a

Cuban Red Macaw was in 1864. This happened near Zapata Swamp on the southern coast of Cuba.

In 1876 Gundlach wrote that he had seen Cuban Red Macaws. But sightings were rare, and there were only a few birds together. Gundlach collected some birds to breed, but was not successful. He could not save the Cuban Red Macaw from extinction.

Another extinct parrot is the Mythical Macaw. Mythical Macaws were found on the islands of Martinique, Guadeloupe, Dominica, Jamaica, Hispaniola, St. Croix, and Cuba. There are no accurate descriptions of these birds, but one of the first persons to mention them was Ferdinand Columbus. There is no accurate record of why these birds became extinct. Even their name – Mythical – suggests they never existed.

The St. Croix Macaw is another extinct parrot. It is only known from a fossil found near Southwest Cape on St. Croix Island. No one has ever seen this macaw.

# The Puerto Rican Amazon

Many types of parrots are endangered. This means they are close to extinction. The Puerto Rican Amazon is one of the endangered parrots.

The Puerto Rican Amazon has mostly green feathers.

Red feathers cover its throat. A narrow band of red runs across its forehead. Some wing feathers are blue and edged with black. Other wing feathers are green and edged with red and yellow. The Puerto Rican Amazon is about 12 inches long.

In 1836 there were large flocks of Puerto Rican Amazons. In 1864 they were still fairly common. As late as 1903 it was common for children to stay home from school to scare parrots. Why? If the parrots were not scared away they destroyed gardens and farm crops. By 1912 Puerto Rican Amazons had disappeared from the western part of Puerto Rico. And they had become scarce in eastern Puerto Rico.

From February 9 to 29, people sighted 20 Puerto Rican Amazons in forests north of Mayagüez in northeast Puerto Rico. Fifty were seen between March 2 and 11, 1912, near the Mayagüez River. They were still fairly common near Naguabo in eastern Puerto Rico. These places were all close to Luquillo National Forest. This refuge has 28,000 acres of tropical forests and is now a bird sanctuary.

A *census*, or count, of Puerto Rican Amazons was taken in Luquillo National Forest from August 1953 to 1956. A flock of 200 parrots was seen. Some experts believe those Amazons were not just one flock out of many flocks. They believe that flock contained all the Puerto Rican Amazons left.

Many Puerto Rican Amazons were shot to stop them from damaging farm crops and banana trees. Some were hunted for food and feathers. Some were captured to keep as pets. Natives taught these pets words in Spanish. But the

*Because people have destroyed the Puerto Rican Amazon Parrot's habitat, that bird is now endangered.*

main reason they are now in danger of extinction is deforestation–the cutting down of large forest areas.

Puerto Rican Amazons are protected by the Commonwealth of Puerto Rico and the United States government. No hunting of these parrots is permitted. They cannot legally be sold to the pet trade. This has allowed the number of Puerto Rican Amazons to remain stable.

The Amazons' natural enemies are still a danger to them. Hawks attack grown Amazons. Black rats go in their nests and destroy their eggs or eat their chicks.

If there were large numbers of Puerto Rican Amazons, natural enemies would not drive them to extinction. But now that their numbers are so small, they may not be able to survive by breeding in the wild. For this reason, a few Amazons are kept in captivity in Luquillo. There are also several Puerto Rican Amazons at a wildlife center in Maryland. These parrots have become breeding stock. When their numbers grow, they will be released in Luquillo National Forest. It is hoped these birds will produce nestlings in the wild. If they do, this will keep Puerto Rican Amazons from becoming extinct.

# Other Endangered Parrots

The Cuban Conure is another endangered parrot. Cuban Conures have mostly green feathers with some red feathers scattered on their heads and stomachs. These parrots have yellow and olive green feathers on the insides of their wings. They are about ten inches long.

Before 1900, the Cuban Conure had an ideal home on the Isle of Pines. The birds nested in the forest and ate fruits, seeds, nuts, and berries. But so many Cuban Conures were caught and sold as pets that they became extinct on the Isle of Pines in the early 1900s.

There are still some Cuban Conures on Cuba itself. But there are not as many as there were just 30 years ago. The reason for this is the destruction of Cuba's forests for homes, roads, and industries.

A South American parrot that is endangered is the Glaucous Macaw. Glaucous Macaws have mostly greenish blue feathers. Their throats are grayish brown. There is a ring of yellow feathers near their beaks. They are about 28 inches long.

Glaucous Macaws are extinct in Brazil. They are extremely rare in Argentina and very rare in other countries of South America, including Paraguay and Uruguay.

The cutting down of forests in southeastern Brazil was the cause of their extinction there. Now there may be too few Glaucous Macaws in other countries to increase their numbers by breeding.

Some ornithologists believe that Lear's Macaw is part Glaucous and part Hyacinth Macaw (another South American breed). Other experts disagree. Lear's Macaw does look like the Hyacinth, but there are several differences between a Lear's Macaw and a Hyacinth Macaw.

Lear's Macaws are greenish blue. Hyacinth Macaws are

cobalt blue. The feathers near the beaks of Lear's Macaws are shaped like half-circles and are pale yellow. The feathers near the beaks of Hyacinth Macaws are longer, narrower, and a brighter yellow. Also, Hyacinth Macaws are about 39 inches long. They are one of the largest of all parrots. Lear's Macaws are about 30 inches long.

Hyacinths are not in danger of becoming extinct. Lear's Macaws are. Because of their large numbers, Hyacinths can survive by reproducing. However, the population of Lear's Macaws may be too small already to save them from extinction.

The pet trade is one reason for their small numbers. Destruction of their forest habitat is another.

# *Adaptable Parrots*

Monk Parakeets, originally from South America, are alive and well in the United States. Monk Parakeets probably came to the United States as pets. Over time some were probably abandoned by their owners, or escaped. They are about 11 inches long, with green and bluish gray feathers. The largest numbers live in Bolivia, Brazil, and Argentina. They are now established in Puerto Rico and the United States and are very adaptable.

In South America parakeets live in forests, farmlands, and palm groves. In the United States they live anywhere they can build a nest.

In South America they build nests in trees. In the United

States parakeets build nests on utility poles, air-conditioners, farm silos, and house roofs. Their nests are unique among parrots'. Most parrots' nests have only a single chamber. But Monk Parakeets nest together in many pairs. Each pair has its own ''room'' with an entrance tunnel. There are no connections between each pair's nest. Some of these nests are four feet high and two feet wide.

In South America Monk Parakeets eat cereal crops and fruit. In the late 1950s Monk Parakeets destroyed many orchards, fields, and farms in Argentina. The government promised to pay its citizens for every pair of feet they brought in. In one province alone, people brought in almost a half million pairs of feet from Monk Parakeets they had

*In the United States, Monk Parakeets have adapted to living in the wild.*

killed. The government also poisoned the parrots, shot them, and burned their nests. Yet Monk Parakeets still survive.

In the United States they eat from backyard feeders, grains, and fruit crops. The Bureau of Sport Fisheries and Wildlife believes Monk Parakeets could become a menace to farm crops in the United States. The government wants to protect crops by keeping Monk Parakeets under control.

The government tries to help other species survive. Twenty-nine Thick-billed Parrots were released in the Chiricahua Mountains in 1987. The parrots had been in captivity for several months. People wondered if the parrots would survive. Would they find food and water? Could they protect themselves from their enemies? Would they go back to Mexico?

Money to pay for a project to observe them came from schoolchildren, zoos, bird clubs, and other wildlife groups. Some money came from as far away as England.

Radio transmitter collars were fitted on the parrots. This was done to keep track of them. The Thick-billed Parrots adapted to the wild. Five more were released. Everything went well for several months. Then the transmitters stopped working. Searches for the parrots began. Radio and television stations asked for people to watch for the flock.

Finally a call came in. It was from a man near Phoenix. Phoenix is almost 200 miles from the Chiricahua Mountains. The man said parrots had dropped pine cones on him. They also squawked at him to scare him away. The

Thick-billed Parrots were acting healthy and normal. This is what they do when they sense an enemy is near.

Not all the released parrots in Arizona survived. But many did. The people who released them consider the project a success.

# *Hope for the Future*

President John F. Kennedy said that conservation is "the prevention of waste and despoilment while preserving, improving, and renewing the quality and usefulness of all our resources."

A balanced environment is what would happen in an ideal world. But we do not live in an ideal world. Many times the wrong decisions are made about the environment.

But Monk Parakeets and Thick-billed Parrots proved that there is hope for wildlife. If they can adapt to new homes, others can, too. Many kinds of parakeets have been spotted in the United States. They escaped from their owners or their owners let them go. These parakeets may establish themselves in their new homes, too. This adaptability may help threatened species survive.

People help, also. *Aviculturists* share information on how to protect birds. They also breed birds in captivity to try to keep a species from becoming extinct. Breeding in captivity might have saved the Carolina Parakeet and other extinct birds. But years ago people did not know enough about breeding parrots.

*ter being in captivity for several months, 29 Thick-billed Parrots re released into the wild.*

*Many steps are being taken to help prevent the extinction of other parrots, like the Pink Cockatoos pictured here.*

Government and bird organizations also help. Thousands of acres have been set aside for bird *refuges*. Stricter laws to protect these lands have been passed. Larger fines for importing endangered parrots are given out. By setting up these refuges and enforcing these laws, we will be able to prevent the extinction of other parrots.

*Their ability to adapt to a new environment will help many species, like the Blue and Yellow Macaw, survive.*

# *For More Information*

For more information on extinct parrots, parakeets, and macaws, write to:

The National Audubon Society
950 Third Avenue
New York, NY 10022

# Glossary/Index

**Psittacidae** 10–the family of birds that includes macaws, parakeets, cockatoos, and lories.

**Psittacosis** 22–a serious bird disease first noticed in parrots that had been brought to the United States.

**Quarantine** 22–the isolation of birds in order to stop the spread of disease.

**Refuges** 45–an area of land where birds, plants, and animals can live away peacefully.

**Species** 8, 10, 25, 43–a single, distinct kind of plant or animal.

**Zygodactyl** 11–Having two toes that point forward and two toes that point backward.